SPACE
MYSTERIES REVEALED

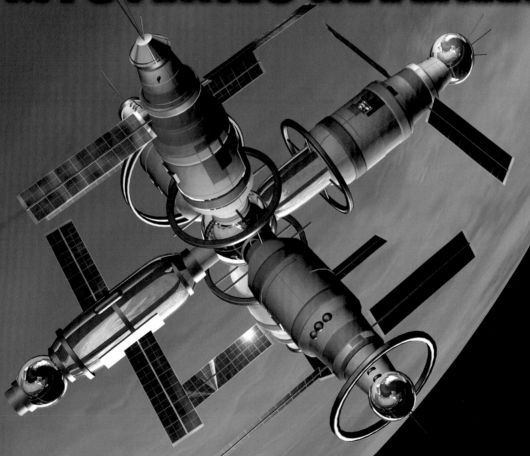

James Bow

Author: James Bow

Editor: Molly Aloian

Project coordinator: Kathy Middleton

Production coordinator: Katherine Berti

Prepress technician: Katherine Berti

Project editor: Tom Jackson

Designer: Paul Myerscough, Calcium Creative

Picture researcher: Clare Newman

Managing editor: Tim Harris

Art director: Jeni Child

Design manager: David Poole

Editorial director: Lindsey Lowe

Children's publisher: Anne O'Daly

Photographs:
Istockphoto: Carmen Martinez Banus: p. 8;
    Stephen Messner: p. 12–13; Metej
    Michelizza: p. 26 (bottom); Dra Schwartz:
    p. 26 (top); Zuki: p. 15 (bottom)
JI Unlimited: p. 14 (bottom)
NASA: p. 9 (top), 14–15, 19, 20, 21, 27, 30
JPL Caltech: p. 10–11
Science Photo Library: Mark Garlick:
    p. 17 (bottom); Mikker Jensen/
    Bonnier Publications: p. 9 (bottom);
    Mehau Kulyk: p. 28 (bottom); Laguna
    Design: p. 29 (bottom); RIA Novosti:
    p. 17 (top)
Shutterstock: Bertrand Benoit: p. 23; Luca Bertolli:
    p. 13 (bottom); Edobric: p. 25; Elen: p. 22
    (bottom); Martine Oger: p. 7; Peresanz:
    p. 4–5; James Thew: front cover; Brent
    Walker: p. 1
Wikimedia: Daein Ballard: p. 22 (top);
    Cosmocurio: p. 28 (top); Neethis: p. 16

Illustrations:
Geoff Ward: p. 11 (top), 29 (top)

Series created by Brown Reference Group

Brown Reference Group have made every attempt to
contact the copyright holders of all pictures used in this
work. Please contact info@brownreference.com if you
have any information identifying copyright ownership.

Library and Archives Canada Cataloguing in Publication

Bow, James, 1972-
    Space mysteries revealed / James Bow.

(Mysteries revealed)
Includes index.
ISBN 978-0-7787-7416-7 (bound).--ISBN 978-0-7787-7431-0 (pbk.)

    1. Astronomy--Juvenile literature. 2. Solar system--
Juvenile literature. I. Title. II. Series: Mysteries revealed
(St. Catharines, Ont.)

QB46.B69 2010   j520   C2009-906260-7

Library of Congress Cataloging-in-Publication Data

Bow, James.
  Space mysteries revealed / James Bow.
      p. cm. -- (Mysteries revealed)
  Includes index.
  ISBN 978-0-7787-7431-0 (pbk. : alk. paper)
  -- ISBN 978-0-7787-7416-7 (reinforced lib. bdg. : alk. paper)
  1. Solar system--Juvenile literature. 2. Astronomy--Juvenile
literature. I. Title. II. Series.

  QB501.3.B68 2010
  520--dc22

                              2009042771

Crabtree Publishing Company
www.crabtreebooks.com   1-800-387-7650
Copyright © **2010 CRABTREE PUBLISHING COMPANY**.
All rights reserved. No part of this publication may be reproduced,
stored in a retrieval system or be transmitted in any form or by
any means, electronic, mechanical, photocopying, recording, or
otherwise, without the prior written permission of Crabtree
Publishing Company. In Canada: We acknowledge the financial
support of the Government of Canada through the Book
Publishing Industry Development Program (BPIDP) for our
publishing activities.

Printed in the U.S.A./122009/BG20091103

Published in Canada
Crabtree Publishing
616 Welland Ave.
St. Catharines, Ontario
L2M 5V6

Published in the United States
Crabtree Publishing
PMB 59051
350 Fifth Avenue, 59th Floor
New York, New York 10118

Contents

Introduction

Astronomers are scientists who study space. The more they learn about the universe, the more questions we have. But scientists love solving mysteries.

Long ago, people believed that the Earth was at the center of the **universe**. The Sun, the Moon, the **planets**, and all stars moved around Earth. But there was a problem: the planets did not follow the rules. They got bigger and smaller and sometimes went backward!

Everything under the Sun

In 1543, Polish astronomer Nicolaus Copernicus realized it made more sense if the Sun was at the center. The Earth, he said, was just a planet moving around the Sun, like Venus, Jupiter, and the others. Many people did not like Copernicus's idea. To them, Earth had to be at the center of everything. However, Copernicus used math to show he was right.

> **"Finally we shall place the Sun himself at the center of the universe."**
>
> **Nicolaus Copernicus**

planets Large globes of rock, ice, and gas that move around a star

△ We cannot visit the stars. Everything we know about them comes from observation.

New questions

The idea of the Sun at the center led to many more questions that needed answers. This book looks at some of today's mysteries of the universe and our place in it. How big is the universe? When did it begin, and are we alone?

AMAZING!

Space begins 62 miles (100 km) above Earth at a point named the Kármán Line. Here, Earth's air is too thin for a plane's wings to work properly. You will need a rocket to fly any higher.

How did the universe begin?

The universe was very different 13.7 billion years ago. Every planet, star, and galaxy in the universe squished into a space the size of a seed. Then came the Big Bang!

During the Big Bang, the universe exploded—everywhere at once. It is thought to have expanded fast. In a fraction of a second, it grew to almost as big as it is now! For the first few seconds, nothing existed except energy. But as the universe cooled, matter appeared: first **protons** and **electrons**, and then, around 200,000 years later, they joined together to form clouds of hydrogen gas.

Pulled together

Gravity pulled the gas into the first stars, which combined hydrogen atoms to form all the other **elements**. When the first stars reached the end of their lives and exploded, new stars and planets formed from the dust and gas left behind. The Sun and our own planet formed about eight billion years after the Big Bang.

The universe formed in the Big Bang. What was there before? Nobody knows.

AMAZING!

In 1964, astronomers discovered radio waves coming from space. The waves were coming from all directions. They realized the waves were the last bit of "noise" left over from the Big Bang.

elements The simple substances that make up almost everything in the universe

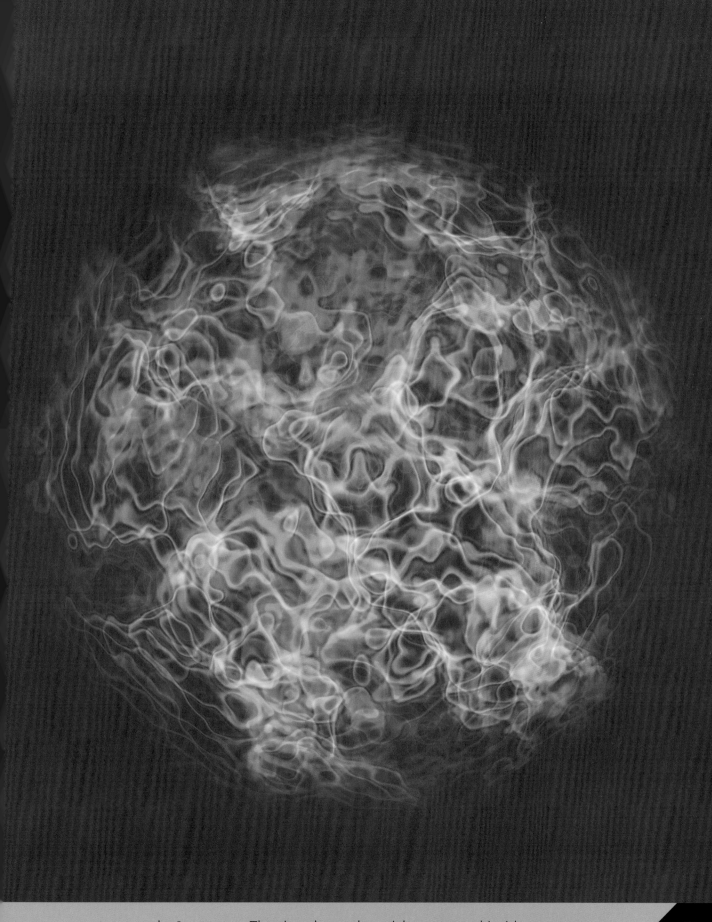

How big is the universe?

The universe is 27 light-years wide. A light-year is the distance a beam of light travels in one year. That is 5,878,625,373,184 miles (9,460,730,472,581 km). The most distant light that we have been able to see took about 13.5 billion years to get here. That starlight is traveling away in the opposite direction, as well, so that makes the universe 27 billion light-years across.

The lens of a telescope scoops up light so you can see faint stars that are too far away to see with your eyes alone.

2D A way of saying an object has two dimensions; 3D objects have three dimensions

The speed of light is 186,282 miles per second (299,792 km/s). That is fast—but the universe is big. The Sun's light takes eight minutes to reach Earth. The next nearest star is four light-years away, so you are seeing that star as it appeared four years ago. As we look at objects that are farther away, we are looking back into the past. The farther we look, the younger objects get. If we could see far enough, we would be able to see the first light produced by the Big Bang!

◯ The light from these stars has traveled for 13 billion years.

Objects bend the space around them, covering the universe in ripples. ◯

Where is space?

Space is everywhere. It is the framework in which everything—planets, stars, basketballs, and you—is placed. Space has **dimensions**. The first dimension is a single line stretching on for ever. The second dimension adds left and right; if we existed only in **2D**, we would all be completely flat. The third dimension adds height. The fourth dimension is time, in which we can travel in only one direction: forward. Scientists think space has six more dimensions, but we cannot see them. Nothing can ever be outside space— there are no dimensions outside of it.

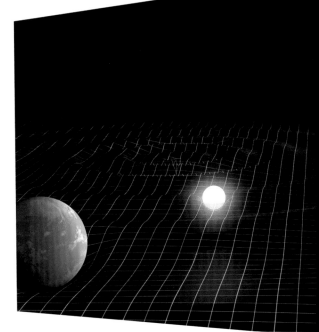

What is dark matter and how do we know it exists?

Scientists have weighed the universe according to how much gravity and **mass** is needed to hold it together. They discovered that the mass we can see covers only one percent of the mass in the universe. The missing 99 percent is dark matter. What is dark matter? Scientists have some ideas: Weakly Interacting Massive Particles, or WIMPs, are tiny bits of matter that are too small to see, but together they weigh a lot. Massive Compact Halo Objects, or MACHOs, are heavy things, such as **black holes** and brown dwarfs. They do not shine, so we cannot see them.

Dark clouds of space rocks and dust might make up some, but not all, of the missing dark matter.

black holes Very small but very heavy objects that pull everything toward them

When a star's hydrogen fuel runs out, the star cools down and swells up by 250 times, becoming a red giant. The biggest red giants explode and form black holes, but most stars throw off their outer layers, leaving a core about the size of Earth. This bright core is called a white dwarf. White dwarfs gradually cool and eventually become black dwarfs. A black dwarf is so cool that it no longer shines. The time it takes for a white dwarf to become a black dwarf is longer than the age of the universe, so no black dwarfs exist—yet.

Our Sun will end up as a black dwarf— in about a billion billion years! ⬤

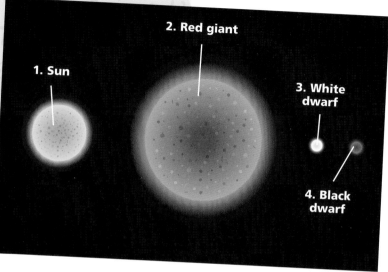

1. Sun

2. Red giant

3. White dwarf

4. Black dwarf

Where is the center of the universe?

There is no center. The universe is expanding everywhere at once, and the distance between stars is getting larger. Earth is like a dot on the surface of a balloon that is being blown up. We see stars moving away in all directions. But wherever you are in the universe, it looks like you are at the center.

mass A measure of how much material, or matter, is inside an object

Why is the universe getting bigger?

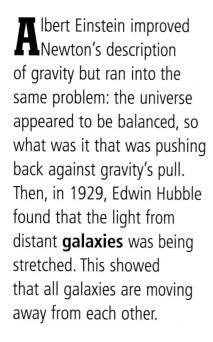

When Isaac Newton discovered how gravity is always pulling objects together, another mystery arose: What kept the universe from pulling in on itself and smashing itself into nothing?

Albert Einstein improved Newton's description of gravity but ran into the same problem: the universe appeared to be balanced, so what was it that was pushing back against gravity's pull. Then, in 1929, Edwin Hubble found that the light from distant **galaxies** was being stretched. This showed that all galaxies are moving away from each other.

> "A man may imagine things that are false, but he can only understand things that are true."
>
> **Isaac Newton**

galaxies Huge groups of stars that gather together in vast swirls and clouds

⬆ The universe is on the move. Stars curve though the sky, night after night, but they are also moving away ⬇ from each other.

Dark energy

The only explanation was that the universe was expanding and always had been. This ended the idea that the universe was unchanging, but it explained why gravity was not pulling everything together. Hubble's observation led scientists to the Big Bang **theory**. Scientists are still figuring out how the universe is changing. The expansion may be getting faster, which could mean that an unknown force, known only as "dark energy," is acting against gravity, pushing everything farther apart.

How can we see our own galaxy?

Imagine trying to describe your neighborhood just by looking out your bedroom window. Studying our own galaxy, the Milky Way, is like that. We are able to see some of our galaxy in the night sky. The Milky Way appears as a cloudy strip full of stars that runs across the sky. It is an edge-on view into the center of our galaxy.

The Milky Way galaxy is in the shape of a whirlpool. ▶

HISTORY EXPLAINED

The milky appearance of the Milky Way is why we created the word *galaxy*. *Galactos* is a Greek word meaning "milk path." Until 1610, the Milky Way was thought to be a cloud. In that year, a great Italian scientist called Galileo Galilei looked at the "cloud" with his homemade telescope (right). He saw the milky appearance was produced by countless stars crammed together.

orbiting Circling a larger, heavier object along a path fixed by gravity

Where are we in the universe?

The Sun is one of 300 billion stars in the Milky Way. The galaxy has spiral arms that sweep around it. Our star is half way down one of the arms, about 26,000 light-years from the center. The Milky Way is one of 40 galaxies in the Local Group, a cluster that is 10 million light-years across. The Local Group is a small part of the Virgo Supercluster, which contains several thousand other galaxies. There are millions of **superclusters** in the universe!

Earth is the third of eight planets **orbiting** the Sun. Astronomers think that half of all stars have planets of their own.

What would happen if the Sun was not there?

Without the Sun, you would not be here to read this. The Sun gives the light that plants need to grow and the heat that everything needs to live. Without the Sun, the oceans would turn to ice and even the gases in the air would freeze. The Sun's pull of gravity also keeps us in the **solar system**. Without it, Earth would float through the emptiness of space.

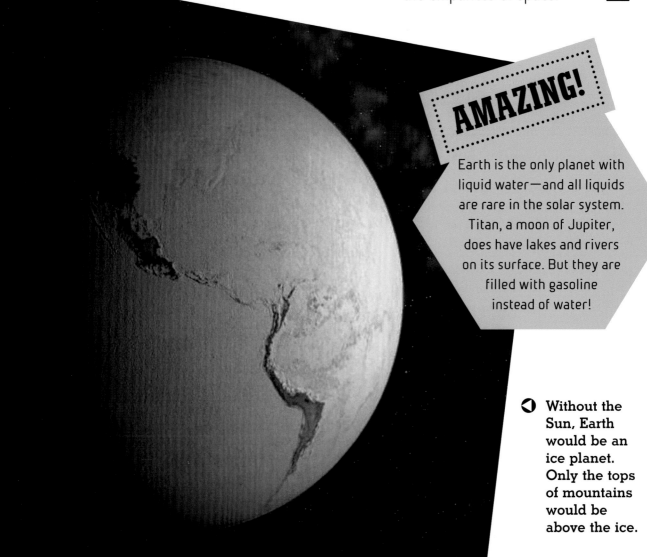

AMAZING!

Earth is the only planet with liquid water—and all liquids are rare in the solar system. Titan, a moon of Jupiter, does have lakes and rivers on its surface. But they are filled with gasoline instead of water!

Without the Sun, Earth would be an ice planet. Only the tops of mountains would be above the ice.

greenhouse effect The way carbon dioxide in the air makes a planet warmer

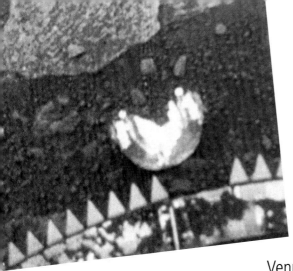

What happens when a probe lands on Venus?

⚫ One of the few probes to land on Venus sent back this picture before breaking down.

Venus crushes space probes like tin cans. The air is so thick with gases that the pressure at Venus's surface is like standing under a half a mile (804 m) of water. Carbon dioxide in the air creates a **greenhouse effect**, and Venus is hotter than an oven. Plastic on the space probe begins to melt, and its computers short circuit. The probe is damaged further as it hits clouds made of acid.

SCIENCE EXPLAINED

⚫ When the Sun turns into a red giant, Earth will become a red hot planet covered in lava.

About 3 billion years from now, the Sun will expand into a red giant, consuming the planets Mercury and Venus. Earth will become the first planet in the solar system, and the giant Sun's heat will blast all life from the face of the planet. However, the outer planets will become much warmer. If humans are still around, we may make new homes on Mars or the moons of Jupiter and Saturn.

When will we live on other planets?

It has been almost 40 years since people last walked on the Moon. Since then, space exploration has been done by robots.

The United States is working on creating new rockets to take people to the Moon in 2020. After that, the spacecraft might take crews to Mars.

Water supply
A flight to Mars and back would take more than two years—with one year living on the planet. The Mars base would need a lot of **resources**, especially water. If Mars has water or ice under the ground, colonists could use it to make oxygen and rocket fuel. Other places with water include the **dwarf planet** Ceres and Jupiter's moons Callisto and Europa.

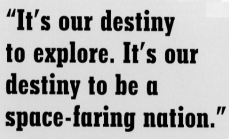

"It's our destiny to explore. It's our destiny to be a space-faring nation."

Eugene Cernan (last man on the Moon)

dwarf planet A large object that orbits the Sun that is too small to be a planet

AMAZING!

Mars's gravity is one third of Earth's. You would be three times lighter there than on Earth. People born on Mars will grow up taller and thinner than their Earth cousins and be able to jump several feet into the air.

A Mars colony might be home to miners looking for minerals or scientists searching for alien life.

How does a flag fly on the Moon?

When Apollo 11 astronauts planted an American flag on the Moon, millions of people saw it stand out straight and flutter as if in a wind. But the Moon has no air—and no wind. The flag stood out because of an L-shaped pole that held it by the side and along the top. What about the flutter? When the astronaut twisted the pole into the Moon's dust, the flag twisted around, too. With no air resistance to slow it down, that twisting went on for a long time, making it look as if the flag was flying.

◀ **Buzz Aldrin stands beside a fluttering American flag on the Moon in 1969.**

radiation Waves containing energy, which includes light, heat, and X rays

How do astronauts survive in space?

Astronauts must wear space suits. The suits protect them from flying dust and deadly **radiation** from the Sun. The suits have 12 layers of clothing, and inside they are filled with breathable air. There is a **vacuum** outside the suit. Without suits, the oxygen in the body leaks out, and the astronaut passes out. After about 90 seconds, the skin freezes, the blood begins to boil away, and the heart fails.

⊘ This spacesuit has a jet pack so the astronaut can fly around the spacecraft.

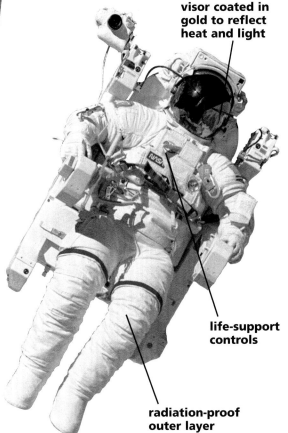

visor coated in gold to reflect heat and light

life-support controls

radiation-proof outer layer

AMAZING!

Three rovers went to the Moon (above). They had electric vehicles: gasoline engines will not run where there is no oxygen for them to burn. The tires were woven aluminum wires with titanium grips.

Could we live on Mars?

The air on Mars is thin and mostly carbon dioxide, which is poisonous to humans. Mars is also a very cold planet. However, there is a way of making Mars warmer and making the air suitable to breathe. The first thing needed is water. If there is not enough water buried in the planet's rocks, then icy **comets** could be made to crash into Mars, creating oceans and rain clouds. The thicker atmosphere that results can trap the Sun's heat, raising temperatures. Then we can seed the oceans with **algae** from Earth, which will release the oxygen we need to breathe.

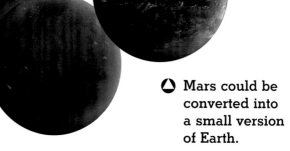

⬤ Mars could be converted into a small version of Earth.

Have aliens landed on Earth?

Probably not. Even light takes four years to travel from the nearest star to Earth. An alien starship would take hundreds of years to reach us. Unless someone finds a way to travel faster than light, we will not be meeting aliens anytime soon.

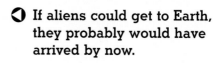

◖ If aliens could get to Earth, they probably would have arrived by now.

algae Tiny plantlike life-forms that live in water

SCIENCE EXPLAINED

It is thought that half of all stars have planets, but only one in every 200 have rocky planets like Earth, where life could exist. A tiny fraction of those planets might have intelligent life. The chances of a planet having a civilization could be as low as one in a billion. But the Milky Way galaxy has 300 billion stars. So there could be 300 alien civilizations in our galaxy alone!

If there are any alien civilizations out there, they would have taken millions of years to grow—just like our civilization on Earth.

comets Balls of ice from the edge of the solar system that fly close to the Sun

What is time travel?

Time is just another dimension, like length or height. If we could learn to move around in time in the same way that we move in space, we could travel to the future and into the past.

A wormhole is a bend, or **warp**, in space. It is a shortcut between two places that are normally distant from each other—in space or time!

Time is linked to space: The faster you travel through space, the slower you move through time. This has been proven with clocks flown at high speeds on planes. When they land, the clocks are running slightly behind others left on the ground. The speed of light is the speed limit of the universe, and if you could travel that fast through space, you would not move at all in time. So, the crew of a spaceship moving at the speed of light would not age on a journey. But on their return to Earth, the crew would find that many years had past at home—they would be time travelers.

"If we could travel into the past, history would become an experimental science."
Carl Sagan

experimental A type of science that performs tests on nature to see how it works

AMAZING!

Wormholes might be a connection between a black hole and a white hole. Black holes pull in everything, including light. Time is switched around in white holes: They give out light and perhaps whole stars!

In 1905, Albert Einstein wrote his famous equation, $E=mc^2$. It explains how energy (E) and matter (m) are two forms of the same thing, and you can change one into the other and back again. The speed of light (c) is the link between the two. The equation says huge amounts of energy are locked away in small masses. That is why a single nuclear bomb can release so much devastating energy.

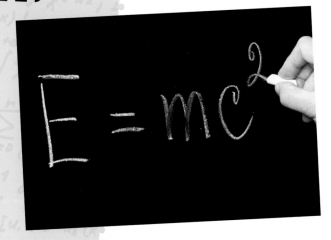

Does gravity travel faster than light?

Gravity is the force that keeps us on the ground and holds the planets in orbit around the Sun. The force travels at the speed of light. If the Sun disappeared there would be no gravity pulling on Earth. We would spin away out of the solar system—but not until eight minutes later. That is how long it would take for the change in the Sun's pull to reach us.

◀ Earth's gravity pulls on us instantly, but we fall to the ground more slowly—air resistance slows our fall.

microgravity The tiny gravity force produced by a spacecraft pulling on the crew inside

● Astronauts must learn how to live in weightlessness.

Will people born in space be able to live on Earth?

Probably not. You are **weightless** in space, and Earth's gravity has a lot to do with how our bodies develop. Astronauts who stay in space a long time see their muscles become weak and their bones get thinner. People born into **microgravity** would have small hearts and would be too weak to walk upright. If they fell over, all their bones would smash into pieces as they hit the ground!

AMAZING!

On Earth, your blood sinks to your feet and your heart works to pump it back up to your head. The heart does the same in space—but it does not need to. Astronauts' faces get puffy with blood, while their legs become very thin.

What would happen if you went into a black hole?

⬇ During "spaghettification" your body would keep stretching forever.

The pull from a black hole is so strong that the gravity pulling on your feet is much higher than the force on your head. Your body would be stretched out by "spaghettification." Black holes also affect time. People watching you fall in would see you freeze in time when you reached the edge. But from your point of view, everything would speed up as the future of the universe passed you in a flash.

constellation A group of stars used on maps of the night sky

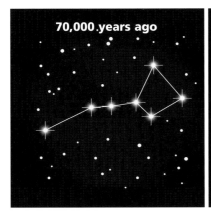
70,000 years ago

Today

70,000 years in the future

Do constellations break apart?

⬤ The stars in the Big Dipper are slowly moving in different directions.

A **constellation** is just a pattern of stars that we have made up. The stars in the group may be in different parts of the galaxy—and the constellation would look completely different from another star system. Stars also move. For example, the Big Dipper constellation may look the same night after night, but in many thousands of years it will be unrecognizable.

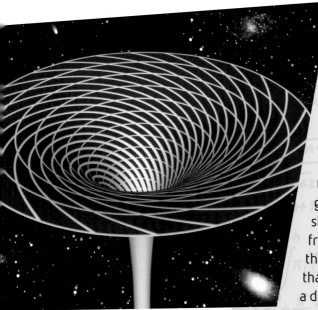

SCIENCE EXPLAINED

To blast off from Earth into space, a rocket must move at seven miles per second (11 km/s). This is the escape **velocity**. The escape velocity of a black hole is 186,282 miles per second (299,792 km/s)—the speed of light. That means that even light cannot escape from the black hole's gravity. That is why they are black—they do not shine at all. The black hole's huge gravity comes from the mass at its center. This object is smaller than a pinhead, but it weighs several times more than the Sun. That huge weight warps space into a deep hole (left) that nothing can escape from.

Space Facts

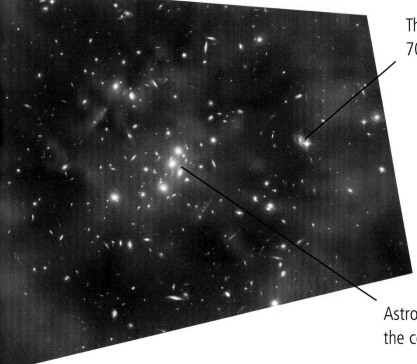

The number of stars in the universe is 70,000,000,000,000,000,000,000.

Astronomers have found snow on top of Venus's mountains. The snow is not made from ice. It is made from chemicals containing the metal lead.

Astronomers are finding black holes at the center of galaxies—even our own.

Find Out More

Books

Space Mysteries by Steve Parker. Raintree Steck-Vaughn, 2002.

Once Upon a Starry Night: A Book of Constellation Stories by Jacqueline Mitton, National Geographic, 2003.

Superman's Guide to the Universe by Jackie Gaff. DK Publishing, 2003.

Web Sites

Sloan Digital Sky Survey
http://skyserver.sdss.org/dr1/en/proj/
basic/universe/

Imagining the Tenth Dimension
www.tenthdimension.com/medialinks.php

National Geographic Space
http://science.nationalgeographic.com/
science/space.html

Glossary

2D A way of saying an object has two dimensions

algae Tiny plantlike life-forms that live in water

black holes Very small but also very heavy objects that pull everything toward them

comets Balls of ice from the edge of the Solar System that fly close to the Sun

constellation A group of stars used on maps of the night sky

dimensions The system used to measure the size and position of an object

dwarf planet A large object that orbits the Sun that is too small to be a planet

elements The simple substances, such as iron and carbon, that make up almost everything in the Universe

experimental A type of science that performs tests on nature to see how it works

galaxies Huge groups of stars that gather together in vast swirls and clouds

greenhouse effect The way carbon dioxide in the air makes a planet warmer

mass A measure of how much material, or matter, is inside an object

microgravity The tiny gravity force produced by a spacecraft pulling on the crew inside

orbiting Circling a larger, heavier object along a path fixed by gravity

planets Large globes of rock, ice, and gas that move around a star

protons and **electrons** The tiny charged particles arranged inside every atom

radiation Waves containing energy, which includes light, heat, and X-rays

resources The raw materials people need to survive and make things

solar system The Sun and the planets and other objects that orbit around it

superclusters Collections of galaxy clusters or galaxy groups

theory A scientific idea that is trying to explain how something works

universe The space that contains everything that exists

vacuum Space that is completely empty; it contains nothing, not even air

velocity The speed of an object in one direction only

warp A curve in space that can bring two distance points right next to each other

weightless How you feel when there is no gravity pulling you down

Index